IT'S TIME TO LEARN ABOUT CHACMA BABOONS

It's Time to Learn about Chacma Baboons

Walter the Educator

Silent King Books
A WhichHead Entertainment Imprint

Copyright © 2025 by Walter the Educator

All rights reserved. No part of this book may be reproduced in any manner whatsoever without written per- mission except in the case of brief quotations embodied in critical articles and reviews.

First Printing, 2024

Disclaimer

This book is a literary work; the story is not about specific persons, locations, situations, and/or circumstances unless mentioned in a historical context. Any resemblance to real persons, locations, situations, and/or circumstances is coincidental. This book is for entertainment and informational purposes only. The author and publisher offer this information without warranties expressed or implied. No matter the grounds, neither the author nor the publisher will be accountable for any losses, injuries, or other damages caused by the reader's use of this book. The use of this book acknowledges an understanding and acceptance of this disclaimer.

It's Time to Learn about Chacma Baboons is a collectible early learning book by Walter the Educator suitable for all ages belonging to Walter the Educator's Time to Eat Book Series. Collect more books at WaltertheEducator.com

USE THE EXTRA SPACE TO TAKE NOTES AND DOCUMENT YOUR MEMORIES

CHACMA BABOONS

In Africa, both far and wide,

It's Time to Learn about
Chacma Baboons

Where mountains stand and rivers glide,

A clever monkey calls its home,

Through trees and grass, it loves to roam.

The Chacma Baboon, so bold and smart,

With hands so strong and mind so sharp,

It climbs and jumps and runs so fast,

In family groups that always last.

With fur so brown and tails so long,

They chatter, bark, and sing their song.

Their faces dark, their eyes so bright,

They watch the world from morning light.

They love to eat both fruit and seeds,

But bugs and eggs will fill their needs.

Sometimes they'll sneak a farmer's crop,

If no one's there to make them stop!

It's Time to Learn about
Chacma Baboons

They live in troops, both big and small,

With leaders strong who guide them all.

Together safe, they watch with care,

For leopards lurking in the air.

Their hands can grab, their feet can grip,

They swing and climb and rarely slip.

Through rocky hills and dusty ground,

The Chacma Baboons leap around.

At night, they sleep in trees so high,

Or cliffs where danger can't come nigh.

They huddle close, they keep so warm,

Or cliffs where danger can't come nigh.

They huddle close, they keep so warm,

Through rain or wind, through sun or storm.

They talk in ways we cannot see,

With grunts and barks and calls so free.

A little noise can say so much,

It's Time to Learn about
Chacma Baboons

To warn, to play, to stay in touch.

Some fear baboons when they come near,

But they're just smart, with little fear.

They live their lives both wild and free,

A part of nature's harmony.

So now you know, so big and bright,

These monkeys live with strength and might.

The Chacma Baboons, so brave and wise,

It's Time to Learn about
Chacma Baboons

These monkeys live with strength and might.

The Chacma Baboons, so brave and wise,

It's Time to Learn about
Chacma Baboons

A wonder under Africa's skies!

ABOUT THE CREATOR

Walter the Educator is one of the pseudonyms for Walter Anderson. Formally educated in Chemistry, Business, and Education, he is an educator, an author, a diverse entrepreneur, and he is the son of a disabled war veteran. "Walter the Educator" shares his time between educating and creating. He holds interests and owns several creative projects that entertain, enlighten, enhance, and educate, hoping to inspire and motivate you. Follow, find new works, and stay up to date with Walter the Educator™ at WaltertheEducator.com

www.ingramcontent.com/pod-product-compliance
Lightning Source LLC
LaVergne TN
LVHW051920060526
838201LV00060B/4088